Internet Marketing Lifestyle

Enjoy Increased Income & More Freedom
from Internet Marketing

By Alexander King

Introduction

If you're working full-time as an internet marketer, then congratulations! You have achieved the lifestyle that millions of people around the world have dreamed of and entered a unique group of self-starters who have the drive, motivation and technical understanding to make a living purely online.

Even if you're not yet making your full-time wage from internet marketing, simply understanding the concept enough to be marketing your services, promoting your own website or helping other businesses and individuals makes you a true pioneer. Just a few decades ago, the idea of making money this way was completely foreign and unheard of. This is uncharted territory and we represent an entirely new way of working and of living.

But is it everything you thought it would be?

Are you truly making the most of this unique position that you've created for yourself?

For many of us, the answer to this is unfortunately a big fat 'no'. Internet marketing can be highly stressful and if you aren't prioritizing your own wellbeing, health and lifestyle then it can be worse than working in an office 9-5.

If you don't know how to separate your work/life balance, if you are constantly stressing about whether you're going to have enough work, or if you feel completely crushed under a massive workload, then you can find that you never really get a time to relax.

Likewise, if you don't get into a good routine, you can end up working from home in your pj's all day, starting work at 1pm and not finishing until 10pm.

Some internet marketers will meanwhile find themselves selling out and doing work that they take no real joy or pleasure in. It can be a soul-destroying experience to spend all your time trying to help people sell low-quality digital products, or even harmful items like steroids. Then there's the feeling that all the work you're doing is for other people and that you aren't 'progressing' in any meaningful way.

Then there's the tax, which is remarkably stressful.

Then there's the difficult clients who make unrealistic demands and unreasonable complaints.

You can end up tired, out of shape, stressed and constantly overworked as you just try to make ends meet. And when it gets that way, you can find yourself wondering if it was all worth it. You took that big leap, that brave experiment and you became a digital marketer. And now you're worse off than you were before...

The Dream of Internet Marketing

Here's what the internet marketing lifestylecan be, if you know how to do it the right way...

For starters, internet marketing can mean having your own business that you take pride in. Imagine being able to hand out cards with your own branding on them, imagine having your own headed letter paper. Imagine employing staff or freelancers and being successful enough to wear nice suits and drive nice cars. It's a great feeling to be financially successful of course. But being financially successful through your own grit and inventiveness – that's a whole other level.

It's just a fantastic feeling when you're at a party and someone asks you: what do you do for a living? And you get to tell them: "I run my own online business". You'll have your own digital empire and you'll feel like an absolute boss.

Working online can also give you the amazing freedom that comes from being self-employed. I recently decided that I was going to take Wednesdays off. Why? Because I can! This way, I only ever have to work two days in a row and I have a day of complete freedom when everyone else is at work. This allows me to run personal errands (banks and hair dressers are empty) and to enjoy being able to play computer games or go on nice walks without any social commitments either! More importantly, it allows me to work on my own projects. To work 'on' my business rather than 'in' it, so that I always feel a sense of forward momentum and so that I'm always progressing the business.

This freedom also affords you a range of other options. If you are worried about the health implications of a job that involves just sitting down all day for instance, then you can get around this issue by making sure you go to the gym every morning before you start work.

Better yet, you now also have the freedom to work wherever you want. How about becoming a digital nomad and working on the move? You can see the world while working out of small cafes and bars along the beaches. Alternatively, you might decide you like your creature comforts too much and decide to create an awesome home office that you can be highly productive in.

If you take this to the absolute extreme, then you can find ways to streamline your business or to get it to run itself. That way, you can earn a purely passive income, meaning that you'll earn money even when you're sleeping or up in the air flying to your destination. Imagine waking up the next day richer?

About This Book

It's time to change the way that you approach internet marketing and to start choosing the lifestyle you want – instead of having it forced upon you.

In this book, we're going to cover all those aspects of the internet marketer's lifestyle and many more. You'll learn how to find a discipline and a rhythm in your work and how to design the kind of lifestyle you want around it. You're going to see how to maximize your productivity, improve your health, make more money and look and feel like the kind of successful business person you probably dreamed of.

All the while, you'll see how to grow your business and turn it into something incredible so that you never start to feel like you're stagnating.

Better Sleep for Greater Efficiency

You want to start making more out of your life as a digital entrepreneur? You want to find ways to enjoy the work you're doing more, to earn more and to progress more?

To do this, you need to have a vision of what you want to achieve. At the same time though, you need to start making smaller, concrete changes to the way you work every day. You need to be able to see the forest and the trees. If you are a sole trader who is running the show alone, then that makes you both the CEO and the workforce and that puts you in a unique and challenging situation.

The problem is that you can get so swamped by the grunt work that you are never able to think about the logical direction that your business needs to take. That means you're constantly treading water and trying to stay afloat and you're never able to implement the systems that would allow you the free time to start working less or more efficiently.

This is how many people who work online find themselves stuck in a vicious cycle of trying to get work done without having the time to look after themselves or enjoy life.

Ironically though, to give ourselves time to focus on the big picture, we first need to hone in on the smallest of details. You probably know you're overworked and you probably know that you should drop the clients you have. You're probably aware that there are likely to be higher paying clients out there who could help you to earn more while working less! But if you've been too afraid to drop or negotiate with your current clients until now, chances are that you aren't about to change any time soon.

We need a solution and that solution is to look at the way you are handling your current work load. Because I'm willing to take a bet that you could be more effective and more efficient. If you're currently starting work at 1pm or even 10am, then you are wasting hours of your day. Likewise, you may well be struggling with things like procrastination or distractions. Perhaps you find yourself constantly interrupted by phone calls, or struggling to stop playing Doom every morning for the first few hours before you do anything useful.

Likewise, there's a good chance that the right technology or even a change in the way you present yourself could help you to get a bit more done. And that will buy us the time we need in the short run to start implementing change.

It's time to look at how you work and if you're approaching your days in the best way possible.

The Importance of Discipline

When you are the boss, it is mighty easy to let lifestyle go to pieces and to find yourself a bit 'all over the place' as you try to instill structure and discipline in your own routine.

But if you're starting work at 10am and finishing it at 10pm, then you're not being as productive as you could be. If you often find yourself finishing work at 1am, then you need to seriously reconsider your approach. Not only is this going to prevent you from being able to enjoy time with your friends and family but it will also come across as unprofessional to your clients. Do you really want to work with someone who is constantly handing work in minutes before the deadline?

Not only that, but you will find yourself constantly tired, strung out and less effective as a result.

The solution is to start instilling discipline. That means that you wake up at a set time in the morning and begin work by a set time too. Likewise, it means that when you're working, you're working. That means no playing games, watching TV or making personal calls.

How to Fix Your Sleep

The first thing you're going to do then is to try and fix your sleep so that when the alarm goes off, you have the will power to spring out of bed and get straight to work (or the gym). This takes a lot of mental discipline but that's part of the point: this will cultivate your discipline and make you a generally more effective and productive person. If you can leap out of bed at 7am when your body is screaming for you to hit snooze... well then you can do anything!

But it starts with getting enough sleep so that you have more energy and will power to begin with. This is something that is very 'in-vogue' right now and all manner of blogs and websites will discuss the topic of 'sleep hygiene' at length.

There are any number of different things you can do to make sure your sleep is deeper, more restful and more effective.

The first is to turn off your phone one hour before bed and to stop looking at it. Same goes for computers, laptops or anything else. For starters, looking at bright screens will cause the release of the stress hormone cortisol which works against the sleep hormone melatonin. The more cortisol you have in your system, the less melatonin you will produce. At the same time, phones and other devices are stressful in themselves. They are stressful because we associate them with important calls, with angry clients and with work. But they're also inherently stressful in the biological sense. That's because they're filled with things designed to trigger arousal and thereby get our attention. These include things like flashing lights, loud noises and bold writing written in red.

Turn it off and your body will start to relax more – especially if you combine this with a bit of reading to help calm the mind and simultaneously make your eyes weary so that you start to feel ready for bed. When it's this time of night there is no reason not to turn off your phone, people will simply assume you went to bed an hour earlier.

Of course, you need to make sure that your bed is comfortable and supportive and you need to ensure that the room is both dark and quiet while you're trying to doze off. Look at getting blackout curtains and remove or cover up anything that has an LED light throughout the night.

Also important is to consider the temperature. We tend to sleep more heavily and deeply when we are slightly cool, so consider leaving a window ajar to stop yourself tossing and turning in the night. A warm shower will also make a difference to your ability to sleep. This helps to relax the muscles and encourages the release of melatonin. Better yet, it helps the body to 'self-regulate' its temperature during the night.

You also need to think about what you're doing during the day. Making sure you get fresh air, exercise and sunlight will help you to sleep much better and thus wake up more refreshed.

Still struggling to doze off into a deep rest? One powerful supplement you can use is vitamin D. Vitamin D is produced in the body naturally when we are exposed to sunlight and this has many key roles in the body – largely revolving around the regulation and production of other hormones. Vitamin D can help to raise levels of melatonin at pertinent times, as well as testosterone giving you more energy. Unfortunately, most of us don't get anywhere near enough sunlight and thus we are severely deficient in vitamin D!

Because vitamin D is associated with sunlight, it can help the body to maintain its circadian rhythms – the rhythms that tell us when to feel tired, when to feel hungry, etc. Take this supplement in the morning and you should find you sleep better and feel recharged and rejuvenated. More recent studies also show that it is highly effective at preventing colds and flu – potentially even more effective than vaccines and medications! This is an important bonus seeing as a nasty cold or flu can completely ruin your productivity for days.

The other powerful supplement I'm going to recommend is magnesium threonate. This is a supplement that you can take just before bed if you are someone who struggles to get to sleep and you should find that it helps you to drop off very quickly.

Magnesium is a mineral we get in our diet and that once again is an important ingredient for a range of processes in the body. In fact, magnesium plays a role in over 300 different chemical reactions throughout the body.

Magnesium is highly effective at encouraging sleep and can put us into a slightly dopey and restful state. In fact, magnesium is the reason that many of us associate milk with sleep! It also happens to be a powerful muscle relaxant, thanks to its ability to remove calcium from the muscles cells (which is involved in the contraction of muscle). Magnesium is also crucial for testosterone production that happens during the night.

Magnesium is equally as effective as melatonin supplements for many people but without the negative side effects or risk of dependence. What's more, it also has a range of other health benefits, making it an all-round great supplement.

Magnesium threonate is beneficial because it is more readily absorbed into the brain. It has also been shown to enhance learning by improving a function called 'brain plasticity'. This is what allows the brain to form new connections and to grow new neurons!

Get Out of Bed on Time, Every Time

The next thing you need to do is to make sure that you are waking up when the alarm goes off. One powerful tip I have in this regard, is to wake yourself up in stages.

NEVER hit snooze. The temptation is great but you will almost always feel more tired when you do rather than more refreshed. You might find that you lack the will to simply jump out of bed though, which is why the better solution is to get up in stages. For example, why not sit up and check your phone for messages? We are often told not to look at our phones first thing in the morning, but if this is something you can look forward to doing, then it will be enough to motivate you to sit up just slightly.

Likewise, you might find that you can motivate yourself to sit up a little and talk to your partner. Or to turn on the TV.

This takes very little effort but by taking this small step, you will start to come around. In 10 minutes, it will feel easier to get up than to go back to sleep!

A Powerful Tool for Waking Up

We can once again augment this with the right tool. In this case, we're talking about a 'daylight alarm'. This is an alarm attached to a powerful light that is designed to mimic the wavelength of the sun and to get gradually brighter as it becomes morning.

The idea is that this lamp will simulate the rising of the sun in the morning, gradually getting lighter and thereby stirring you out of bed. The devices are designed to treat those who suffer with 'SAD' or 'Seasonal Affective Disorder'. However, they can be useful for helping anyone who struggles with their energy levels in the morning for two reasons:

first, they rouse you into a lighter stage of sleep before the alarm goes off, thereby making you feel less 'jolted' when you wake up (a phenomenon called 'sleep inertia'). What's more, is that when you do wake up, the room feels bright and this boosts your energy in a big way compared with waking up into a dark room and fumbling for an unnatural feeling lamp!

Cultivating Discipline

Okay so now you're up, what next?

It's up to you what time you get up and how long you need to come around. Most likely, this will be linked with other lifestyle commitments and requirements. Once you've decided to sit down and work though, the next challenge is to work and not get distracted by other things or put off working while procrastinating.

The biggest issue with procrastinating is that it's not even restful or fun. When most of us procrastinate, it means we will spend our time browsing the web absent minded, playing mobile games or otherwise just generally wasting time while feeling stressed about the fact that we're not working. Now think how much nicer it would be to work solidly in the morning and then to have a few hours at the end of the day to relax and to really unwind and enjoy your freedom!

So how do you encourage yourself to dive straight into work and to keep working until you have finished everything? The following tips will help you do that.

Separate Your Days into Blocks

The first point is to make sure that you do have periods of relaxation and fun on the horizon. If you are setting out to work and your plan is simply to work solidly from first thing in the morning until last thing at night, then your brain is very likely to fight you on that. Unfortunately, most of us do not have complete control over our brains and emotions and when we work against them, that's when we have problems.

If you know that you have 8 hours of solid work ahead with no break in sight, then that is when you are going to struggle to stay focused.

So instead, you're going to separate your day into distinct blocks which will include time for you to relax and unwind.

To do this, you need to think first about what it is you need/want to accomplish that day and how long you have until it's time to sign off. Another piece of useful information is to know roughly how long you tend to take completing any given amount of work.

This in turn will then allow you to work out how long you need to complete each task. With that knowledge, you'll then be able to break each task into several hour slots and punctuate them with periods of rest. Even if that 'rest' is just 10 minutes or 20 minutes, that's enough to give you something to work towards and to give you a break – which is important for your health as much as anything else.

A day might look like this then:

Monday

8am-9am - Workout

9-10am – Work on Guest Posts for Client 1

10am-10.10am – Make Cup of Tea

10.10am-11am – Look for New Clients/Respond to Emails

11am-11.20am – Mid-morning Snack/Magazine

11.20am-2pm – Link Building for 3 Smaller Clients

2pm-2.30pm – Lunch/Episode of Favourite TV Show

2.30pm-4pm – Site Design

4pm-4.10pm – Make Coffee

4.10-5.30pm – Start Tomorrow's Work

5.30pm-6.30pm – Time to Relax

This now gives you a day that is filled with lots of large work projects but also gives you opportunities to relax and unwind and to catch your breath. Starting work isn't so bad when you know that between the hours of 11am-11.20am, you'll be able to relax with a cup of tea. And working again until 2pm isn't so bad when you know you've got half an hour for lunch.

While many of us think that the best way to be productive is to dive straight into work and give ourselves no breaks, this is actually the worst thing you can do as you'll find your brain 'fights' that and urges you to do more fun or relaxing things. It might feel indulgent to be taking hours' worth of breaks and snacks but you probably normally break for longer than that in a day. Only now you're enjoying that time off, using it to recharge your batteries and making it more predictable and scheduled.

Something else you might have noticed here is that I've gone as far as to schedule when to drink cups of tea and coffee. (Pro tip: a coffee at 4pm is a way to pick yourself up during a time when the body is most tired and lethargic after work!)

This is quite important and will help you to be much more productive. Why? Because little breaks to make tea can take you out of the 'zone' and represent a much bigger break in your workflow than you realize. If the first thing you do is make tea or coffee, then have a snack, then answer emails... it can quickly get to 10.30am and you still haven't achieved anything! This is a very crushing feeling and it's enough to set you back much further.

So instead, start working on something useful and important right away and that way you'll be able to get your day off to a great start. Come 10.30am, you'll already have a big 'win' under your belt which will set you up for the day ahead.

Another tip to making this plan work, is to make sure that the scheduled time slots for each piece of work are longer than you think they'll probably need to be. In other words, if a piece of work normally takes you 2 hours to complete, then schedule it to take 2.30 hours. Why? Because that way you will trust in the system and feel like you really can take those breaks. If your work is constantly down to the wire, then it will hurt the quality, it will make you feel stressed about finishing it and you'll risk not getting everything done that you need to.

Jump Straight into Work

The next question is what you should be setting as your first task for the day. And the answer to that is that ideally, you should make the task something that is relatively easy and fun.

The hardest part of getting into the flow when working, is putting yourself in that mental state to begin with. Once you're going, it's relatively easy to maintain. It's getting to the point where you're going in the first place that's hard!

If you make your first task one that is overwhelming, unpleasant and very dull, then chances are you'll find yourself putting it off, making excuses and procrastinating. But if you make it something that is relatively easy/fun, then you might find yourself jumping into it much more effectively.

That said, do also try to move the more crucial and urgent work toward the start of the day. The aim is that if you reach burnout by 3pm, you should already have accomplished all the absolutely most urgent tasks that you need to complete. Again, this buffer will then allow you to put more trust in the system.

Another useful tip in this regard is to 'half finish' a project the day before. Start writing a piece of content, or an email, or start designing a website/handling some on-site SEO. This will make it much easier to dive back in right away the next day and the reason for that is that is that we don't like unfinished business. It is human nature to want to complete a piece of work that is already started and this means you'll be able to dive in with a lot less resistance.

Finally, if you experience the equivalent of 'writers' block', then the best way to overcome this is to force yourself to do some work. Whether that means designing a few buttons or just writing something down, don't worry if you're lacking inspiration and the work lacks quality. The best way to get into the groove is to just start and you can always go back and fix what you wrote/made later.

Try following these pointers for the next few days and see how it improves your workflow. What you should find, is that you're able to start earning back some time in your day and thereby to get yourself some free time. From there, we can start looking at how to improve the quality of your business and of your life!

Hardware and Location

Want to upgrade your work experience? Want to get more work done and enjoy doing it more?

An easier way achieve that is to upgrade the hardware that you're working with! You will use this every single day. So why not make sure that it is a pleasant experience and that you are able to get as much work done as possible?

A good place to start is by making an awesome home office.

To begin with, that means getting the right computer that will be powerful enough to handle any software you work with regularly and then some.

Later in this book, I'm going to talk about the importance of self-development: learning new skills in order to advance your capabilities. One example of this is to learn 3D modelling. 3D modelling lets you create stunning 3D logos, video openers and more. It can really add to your repertoire and set you apart from other marketers, or help you to improve your own branding.

To do things like this, you need to have power. That's why I recommend getting yourself a beefy computer – something with an i7 processor that you can overclock to 3++ GHz and something backed up with powerful graphics capabilities. A GTX 1060, 1070 or 1080 will make your machine highly future proof and will make it powerful enough to play all the latest games too.

As a marketer, you will likely be doing a lot of writing – whether that's writing blog content or emails. Either way, it's important to think about how this is going to affect your finger health. You need to make sure you do everything you can to avoid the possibility of RSI (repetitive strain injury) and to do that, you should look at getting yourself a better keyboard.

The best keyboards for writers are 'mechanical keyboards'. These are keyboards with satisfyingly click keys. They last longer than the membrane keyboards found on cheap laptops and they are highly enjoyable to type on. Many people consider the ideal switch for typing to be the Cherry MX Blue switches. I'm also a fan of the rapid fire keyboards that require a little less power and force in order to reach the actuation point.

I recommend trying out a few of these keyboards in store, to make sure that you like the typing experience.

Finally, to round out the experience, I recommend getting an ultrawide monitor. Ultrawide monitors have been shown to boost productivity by as much as 30% and this is because they allow for much more efficient multitasking: letting you have multiple different elements on the screen at once without having to keep switching between tasks. This is also ideal for anyone who works with spreadsheets as you'll be able to stretch them out wide and see lots of columns all on the one screen at once!

A multi-monitor set-up can do similar things but isn't ideal as it means having a large divide in the middle made up of the monitor bevels. Furthermore, having a single monitor means having fewer wires and cables and taking up less space on your desk.

Tips for a Productive Home Office

With your computer in place, you can now start to design the rest of your office around it. A basic key thing to consider in this regard is that the space needs to be comfortable and somewhere that you enjoy working.

A good starting point is to make sure that the office is a separate room in the house. This is important because it will mean that it isn't prone to getting untidy or disorganized (things that can prevent you from feeling relaxed while working). At the same time, you should also make sure that your office is decorated with things that you find inspiring or just want to be around.

You're going to be working here every single day for the most part. So why not turn it into a place that you love to be? That makes you feel inspired and productive? Some lighting can make a huge difference in this way, as can a cool ornament or two.

Try to keep the room tidy and clear too and make sure that you have a large surface to use as your desk and that you have plenty of drawers for storing items in as well.

Working on the Move

While having a powerful computer and a base of operations can also make a big difference to your mental health as an internet marketer, it's also a good idea to create something of a 'mobile command center'. In other words, spend some time collecting all the items you'll need to work productively on the move and make sure that this is also something you look forward to doing.

If you are someone who struggles with staying productive and avoiding distractions – even with the tips we've outlined in this book already – then a good strategy could be to try working in coffee shops. Coffee shops provide free WiFi, power and a place to sit. They also provide coffee, which is ideal for stimulating the brain.

What's more though, is that they are highly conducive to productivity because of their vibe. The quiet chatter of people in the background, the smell of coffee, the other people all beavering away on their various laptops – all of this puts you in a state where you feel ready to be productive.

Better yet, you'll probably find that it's hard to get distracted when you're working in coffee shops. You won't feel like you should be browsing YouTube or playing games because other people can see you! You'll most likely get your head down and work and this is a way to force yourself into that productive state. I used to work in coffee shops every day of the week and while I would spend a fair amount of money on coffee, I found that I got so much extra work done that it paid for itself. Sometimes I would write as much as 30,000 words by working this way! That's how I cultivated my productive mindset and now I'm able to work nearly as effectively from home.

So, what hardware should you consider getting if you want to create the perfect mobile command station?

Look for a computer with great engineering. This should be one that is beautifully made and joyous to hold and work with. Look for a high-resolution display and a comfortable keyboard. Again, you need to want to work on this and to feel great when you do.

I highly recommend the Surface Pro line of devices from Microsoft, or their Surface Books. These computers have high resolutions, they run quickly with decent specifications and they're very light and convenient. The ability to write on the screen with the stylus creates a lot more possibilities for design work and means you can sign off Word Documents and PDFs.

Things like this are small, but they make your business look that much more professional and they make you feel like a better worker too. When I upgraded from my old HP to a Surface Pro, I found myself really looking forward to getting into cafes to work. What's more though, I could now run software like Illustrator and make proper vector images to use as logos. Likewise, I was capable to start sketching designs and I could learn coding in Unity.

The hardware made me feel more professional. It gave me more belief in myself. It extended my capabilities. And for all those reasons, it helped me to start doing better work and earning more. You need to spend to accumulate, and if you can invest in better tech, you will earn more!

This is somewhat like the approach taken by investors. Often, traders will be encouraged to splash out on expensive items and the idea behind this is that it makes them more likely to become big earners! Sounds strange, but by acting like a success, you'll often find you become one.

How to Afford Better Tech

But what if you can't afford better tech like this? Even as an investment? One answer is to take out a loan and a great way to do that is through PayPal. If like most marketers, you are currently getting paid through PayPal, then you'll be able to get a loan through the website called 'PayPal Working Capital'. This isn't the cheapest loan (a credit card loan is a better option in that regard – especially one with 0% APR), but the thing about it is that there's no deadline and the interest is agreed up front as a single fee. That means you can take your time paying it off. Better yet, the repayments are taken directly from your earnings as they come through PayPal.

So, if you normally earn $100 a day and you need to pay back your loan in instalments of 10% of your earnings every day, then you can simply start earning 10% more until the loan is paid off and not even feel it. Better yet, if you struggle to find work or business goes slow for any other reason, you'll not face penalties or see damage done to your credit score.

Better yet, you can also claim this back on your tax as expense. That means that you will get 30% off the cost of new laptops, new software or anything else that you use to upgrade your working experience and work flow. And even better is that this also applies to the interest you're paying, essentially cutting a third off the cost of the loan.

The thing is that most internet marketers like technology – after all, that's why you probably became a marketer to begin with. So, using these tips, you can now start getting all kinds of awesome things that you've always wanted – a smart new phone, a great computer, a fancy keyboard, a beautiful monitor – and not feel the impact financially!

I'm about to take this even further by building an 'office pod' in our garden. This is a beautiful installation that will become a home office and let in plenty of light. It's free standing, made of glass and it will give me lots of space to add a large desk and lots of tech. It's tax deductible, I can buy it through PayPal working capital and it will add a lot of value to my property – so it's a no brainer!

What to Wear for Internet Marketers

We've talked a little about how to upgrade your tech and how this can make you a better digital marketer. But now I want you to consider upgrading your wardrobe too.

This is important for when you meet with clients in person – and especially if you're a marketer who likes to find clients in the real world a lot. It's also great for attending networking events. But you know what else? It's also important for your own sense of achievement and for the 'law of attraction'. They say to 'dress for the job you want, not the job you have' and this is very true. If you currently work unshaven in stained t-shirts, then you aren't going to feel your most productive.

Think of the film Limitless about the man who takes the brain-boosting drug 'NZT' and uses it to become a highly successful trader, author and eventually politician. What's the first thing he does when he takes the pill? He tidies his home, gets a haircut and puts on a suit.

Just like taking breaks, this feels like an indulgence but it is crucial to doing your best work. I recommend taking some time out on a coming weekend and using it to upgrade your wardrobe.

Should You become a Digital Nomad?

Working in coffee shops can make you feel more productive, prevent cabin fever and put you in an environment where lots of people are all doing similar work.

But how about taking this to the next step? How about working while you travel and living the dream? So many of us wish that we were truly free and able to see the world but as an internet marketer, you really can. Imagine being able to see stunning glaciers, views from incredible mountains, the northern lights, the Full Moon Party... imagine sitting in a café watching the world go by while you work on your laptop. That is the dream of being a digital nomad and as an internet marketer, this is something that you can very easily accomplish. But is it right for you?

Nomads: Know Your Options!

Becoming a digital nomad in many ways feels like the ultimate way to 'make the most of life'. We only get one go around on this planet and in that time, there is so much most of us will never see. There's a world out there filled with a variety of cultures, incredible sights and adventures and so much more.

Most of us will never experience any of these things, other than when we're playing Skyrim (which is not the same!). Instead, we spend out days typing away on a computer and our evenings sitting in front of the TV. Meanwhile, we get older and miss out on conversations with strangers on bars set by the beach...

When you put it that way, it's hard to imagine why anyone would not want to become a digital nomad. For the right type of person, this is a truly wondrous experience.

But there are downsides to being a nomad too. For one, this means saying goodbye to all your creature comforts and it means moving away from family and friends. Being constantly on the move means not being able to take a warm bath, or watch your favourite boxset back-to-back. These might not be things that look great on Instagram but they are still things that many of us enjoy and rightly so!

If you will struggle with that and if you'll struggle with not being able to see your best friend, then being a digital nomad might not be for you. Likewise, if you want to grow your business as quickly and well as possible, then you might do better to stay at home. And if you're in a relationship, if you're a parent, then it will be harder too.

But here's the thing: being a digital nomad is just one option. This is just one example of 'lifestyle design' and actually there are many other ways that you can enjoy the benefits of working online and being self-employed.

For example, even if you don't decide to travel constantly, you might just decide to travel a little more. How about going for lots of shorter holidays throughout the year? These days, you can get very affordable flights and stay in Air BnB, so it's affordable. And because you can continue working as you go, you can more easily afford the trip. This way, you can still experience lots of new things and see the world – but without feeling like you have nowhere to call home!

Another option is just to enjoy your own local area more. Working in coffee shops is one thing, but what about working at the local library, on the beach if you live near one, or in an outdoors café? How about in your own garden?

I lived in London, England for 4 years and during this time I would work by the docks sometimes, I would work with views of Big Ben, I would work in huge museums... I was constantly finding places to work that would give me inspiring views while I typed away. When I lived in Bournemouth before that, I would often sit on the beach and work there – or in the bars near the beach.

All this punctuated by regular trips with my friend who was also an internet marketer! One of my favorite working memories was sitting in a café in Zadar, Croatia and drinking beer while listening to some amazing music (Schiller, it turned out). It was lightly raining but warm and we could see people outside passing on the cobbled streets and mountains in the background below. More recently we worked in a Swiss chalet on the side of a mountain!

Creating Work/Life Balance

No matter how much you like your work set-up or how efficient and productive you become, you will still need to consider ways to manage the balance between work and play. This is something that many self-employed people struggle with and it's easy to understand why.

The first and biggest issue here is that when you do work like SEO, writing or web design, you will have the opportunity to effectively earn unlimited cash. Want more cash? Then work a few more hours! It's that simple.

But in doing this, you are now creating a situation where you feel 'guilty' any time you relax and let yourself become calm.

Another problem is the fact that you are working online, which means people can contact you at any time of day. This becomes even more of an issue if those people happen to be based in other countries where they are operating by different time zones!

So, what can you do?

Setting a Budget

From reading the advice that we've shared so far, you might already have noticed something of an irony starting to emerge.

You want to be freer and to have more spare time but the best way to do this is to place more restrictions on yourself! By creating a more disciplined work schedule for instance, you give yourself more time off and let yourself clock out earlier.

Similarly, creating a budget for yourself can ironically help you to feel freer. Look at all your regular income and outgoings and then decide how much money you need to get by. Likewise, think about how much you'd ideally like to save each month, how much you want to spend on treats for yourself and how much money you need to set aside for tax.

This is an important and useful point to consider right now: tax is going to be one of the big stresses you face as an internet marketer or anyone who is self-employed – so get it out the way by setting that money aside immediately.

In fact, a big tip I should share at this point, is to have multiple accounts. Each time you get paid, split the money into a bills account, saving account, tax account and allowance. That way, you'll be able to avoid spending too much and not affording rent, or forgetting to put aside enough for tax at the end of the month.

Oh, and always calculate your tax as soon as possible so you have time to save the amount you need.

This might sound like a tangent but there's a point to it: it allows you to decide how much you need to earn to get the lifestyle that you want. This in turn means that you know how many clients you need to hire and how much you need to charge and that means that you can then decide how late you need to work.

In this way, you are setting your own 'wage' and that means you are setting yourself targets, rather than creating a situation where you feel the need to earn money indefinitely and never stop!

Separating Work and Play

This means that you can now set an amount of work you need to do before you sign off. And ideally, you should also set a time at which you will stop working every day. This might be dictated by other life commitments, or it might just depend on how long it takes you to do the work you need to do.

Either way, you now have an ability to draw a line under a day's work and then stop.

And now you must be strict when it comes to not responding to emails, not taking on more work and not squeezing more in. Remember, down time is what will allow you to work more productively when you return to work.

And after all, what's the point of being a successful entrepreneur if you never have any time to enjoy the spoils of your success?

Another tip to this end is to separate work and play by having a separate work phone and separate work email. This way, you won't be tempted to answer messages when you're not working.

It really is important not to make exceptions here. Once you make an exception once, you can be sure that your clients will think that you should always be available to answer messages or to 'just quickly finish this bit of work'.

They will be sure to take advantage of your free time if they can, which is not because they are malicious, but simply human nature. This must be an iron clad rule and if you do end up working extra hours, don't let them know!

Not reading the emails is also very important. Even if you don't respond to an email, just knowing it's there can be enough to make you stressed and prevent you from being able to properly relax and enjoy your work.

The evenings and the weekends are the time that you are going to use to work on other aspects of your life. This is when you'll build your strength in the gym, it's when you'll develop yourself as a person by travelling, meeting people and reading. It's when you'll recharge your soul. And it's when you'll develop relationships and friends. If you are struggling to find a relationship as an internet marketer, then consider whether you're giving yourself the opportunities you need to meet them!

You might find it can be stressful knowing that you're probably getting urgent messages that you can't see. The answer to this is just to be up-front and honest with your clients. Tell them that you won't answer except for during set hours. Let them know in advance when you plan to go away. And if you're still concerned, set up an autoresponder to ensure they'll get the memo.

When You Need a Little More Cash…

One of the better things about being self-employed though is that aforementioned option to earn more money as and when you need it: to be able to afford whatever you need, just by working a little longer.

This might seem like a sacrifice if you are forcing yourself to work set hours but you can have your cake and eat it yet again. In this case, the option once more comes from the restrictions you've placed on yourself and the fact that you have a set budget.

You know how much you need per month, you know how much you earn per month. Thus, if you find yourself lusting after a new toy or wanting to go on a holiday, you have two options:

1) Save money in your 'daily' budget until you have enough spare to funnel into that thing.

2) Work over time just to afford that one thing. Once you've earned that amount... stop!

This way, you can have anything you want. Just another amazing advantage to being an internet marketer!

Charge More and Work Less

If you are an internet marketer with clients (rather than marketing your own stuff), then you'll have another tricky thing you need to manage: the clients.

Because in many ways, having a client is just like having a boss and that means you have the same commitments and the same requirement to follow instructions and work to someone else's timescale. At the same time though, a client doesn't come with a contract, meaning that they could stop offering you new work at any time.

This can create a situation where you need all the clients you have, just in case one stops working with you. At the same time though, that means you need to be available when they need you, meaning there will inevitably be times when they supply you with too much work and you end up breaking your back to try and get it all finished.

The question is how exactly you deal with this. Another issue is the 'difficult' client. Sometimes, you will get clients that expect too much from you and you will find that clients constantly have problems with your work. Sometimes, they will simply be rude! This can make life very stressful, so again, you must find a way to deal with that problem.

How to Remove Difficult Clients

The first thing you need to do, is to learn how to deal with those difficult clients and thereby make your life easier.

The key here is to have the strength to turn down work. This is something that can be very hard to do and especially if you are an anxious personality type. But it's also very important to prevent yourself doing unlimited amounts of work.

So, what kinds of clients do you turn down? One is the type of client who is making your life hellish. If you keep having to make changes to work that is perfectly acceptable, if you are dealing with rude emails or unreasonable expectations, then you are better off dropping those clients. This is important in fact, as you will ultimately be spending more time on that kind of work while getting less done. Instead, focus on clients that keep things simple for you as that way you can complete more and maybe do more for them. Work for the clients that deserve your work.

This changes the whole mentality too. When you are willing to refuse work, you remember that you don't have a boss. You are working together because you have mutual aims and complimentary skills and resources. If a job is too big or you don't like the way it is being carried out, then be ready to say: 'no thank you'.

Always be polite though. No matter how rude or unreasonable the client is, being rude back is unprofessional and it will burn your bridges in case you ever need future work!

The other kind of client to remove from your workload is the kind that only ever makes very small orders but involves a lot of communication to get them. I have a rule that any client that wants a Skype meeting is probably someone who enjoys 'playing' business, rather than someone who is genuinely a good business partner. Keep communication down and productivity up. Do this by seeking out good clients who have a good working style and by keeping your client roster lean.

Work Less and Get Paid More

Another reason to avoid swamping yourself in unfathomable amounts of work, is that this will give you the freedom you need to take on new projects that pay better. If you are getting paid a certain amount for your work and you have a little more bandwidth to complete more, then you can place adverts that don't need to be desperate. In turn, that means you can charge a little bit more and it won't be the end of the world if you don't get any takers.

Now, once you have several clients all paying a little bit more, you can go on to start getting your existing clients to bid for you. Let them know that your rates have increased and that you now need to charge X amount.

This is scary to do but it's also completely reasonable and normal. And by putting your rates up, you'll be able to earn more or work less. Maybe both!

Try negotiating even if you don't have extra work too. The worst-case scenario is that people say no, in which case you just carry on as you are. If you're nervous about doing this, then a tip for internet marketers is to try offering more for that increased amount. In other words, don't just ask for more money and sour relations – explain how your service is improving as a result.

Setting Realistic Expectations

Another tip for internet marketers that want to avoid being swamped with work, is to set realistic expectations. In other words, don't promise a client you'll get them to the top of Google because that's not something you can guarantee. And likewise, don't promise to complete 10 videos for them per week if that's more than you can accomplish.

A benefit of the business is that you can sell a lot of packages with different services and products involved. You don't need to write hundreds of thousands of words, or to build countless links: you can simply change the package to reflect the kind of work that you are best at and that you personally like doing.

One last tip is that to save yourself from a scenario where all your clients have left you, try to find a few clients that want more work than you can provide. Find a few that will be flexible and take on more work when you have the time. Finally, keep a list of your old clients so that you can use that to offer deals and incentives to get people to hire you. If work is slow, then you can message your old clients and let them know about your discounted packages!

Automation

And if you do get more work than you can handle? The best answer is often to outsource or automate. This might mean just giving your work to someone else and paying them slightly less than you are getting paid to write it. This is where you can start to build up a roster of freelancers, which will give you more spare time to work on other things or relax and which will give you the satisfaction of 'being the boss'.

Tools can also help you to complete work more quickly, as can finding ways to reuse old materials.

Finding Meaning in Your Work

Now you should find yourself enjoying a much better work-life balance and earning more money while earning less. Maybe you're using this newly found freedom to travel, or just to relax a little more!

But what you should also be doing, is taking a step back from your business and deciding on where you want to take it and how you want to grow it.

If you are currently doing link building work for people every day, then chances are that you're going to find yourself feeling rather frustrated and bored with that work. It's not rewarding because you don't know where you're going with it and because you're not doing things you love.

One way to fix this is to go more niche. Instead of being an internet marketer, how about positioning yourself as a 'fitness internet marketer' or a 'fashion internet marketer'. In this way, you help yourself to stand out a bit from all the other marketers and at the same time, you'll now be writing about things you love, dealing with other websites you love and reading about what you love!

Another tip is to develop yourself. We discussed this briefly already but as you start to add new skills to your roster, you'll be able to expand your own services and to grow yourself professionally. You can this way charge more, impress your clients more and get more sense of reward from what you do. Learn to program, learn to design, learn to write – all these skills will make you more well-rounded and open up new doors for you.

Similarly, look at other ways you can generate income, look at ways you want to grow your business and consider using your marketing skills to create your own brand.

This might mean having a brand for your own business. You'll feel much more pride in what you do when you have your own business website, your own business name and a reputation that you're proud of. Plus, this can help to bring a lot more clients to your business without you having to get out there and find them.

Think about expanding too. Look at how you can grow your business, take on new clients and perhaps outsource more of your work – or get in-house staff!

Or alternatively, how about running your own blog? This can work as a brilliant showcase for what you can do, or it can be used to build trust and authority if you are writing about the subject of internet marketing. Most of all though, having a blog will give your business new direction and help you to feel as though you are making progress. You can even feel like something of an internet celebrity, which is a great bonus of working online!

Conclusion

By now, I hope you have some strong ideas and incentives to start changing how you run your business. That means changing the way you handle clients, it means making sure you aren't spending hours procrastinating every morning and it means turning your health and your happiness into top priorities.

Internet marketing is a job that can give you immense freedom, financial success, mild fame and an incredible sense of satisfaction. To get there though, you need to work on your business as well as in it. The journey starts here!